Bygone Days in Burgess Hill

MARK DUDENEY AND EILEEN HALLETT

Mid-Sussex Books

First published in 2003

Mid-Sussex Books
4 Crescent Road
Burgess Hill
West Sussex
RH15 8EG

© 2003 Mark Dudeney and Eileen Hallett
Illustrations © 2003 Mark Dudeney
ISBN 0 9530625 2 X

All rights reserved. No part of this publication may be reproduced,
stored in a retrieval system, or transmitted, in any form or by
any means, electronic, mechanical, photocopying, recording
or otherwise, without the prior permission of the Publisher.

Series Editor: Rose Hill
Editor: M.L.M. Dudeney
Printed in Great Britain by Delta Press, 2 Goldstone Street, Hove, BN3 3RJ

Front cover – **Church Road, January 1915**
The soldiers are members of the London Rifle Brigade which was
billeted in the town shortly after the outbreak of the First World War.
Back cover – **St. Edward's Chapel, Royal George Road, 1936.**

Acknowledgements

The authors gratefully acknowledge the following contributors:

Jean Ball

Maurice Bower

David Butterworth

Patrick Dale

Joan Dew

Jane Hatt

Donald Lever

Bill Lockett

Rose Powell

Joyce Standing

Sources

A Very Improving Neighbourhood,
Ed. Brian Short

Battle over Sussex,
Pat Burgess and Andy Saunders

Burgess Hill,
Hugh Matthews

Burgess Hill About Town Magazine

Daily Mail

Daily Telegraph

Edwin Street and the Victoria Pleasure Gardens,
Mark Dudeney and Eileen Hallett

Evening Argus

Hanningtons,
Sidonie Bond

Mid Sussex Times

Sussex County Magazine

The Story of Burgess Hill Parish Church

The Old Century,
Mark Dudeney (to be published)

The Story of Burgess Hill,
A. H. Gregory

West Sussex Gazette

Why I Went To Prison,
John Charles Bee-Mason, MBE

There was a time when shepherds, having tramped many miles across the South Downs, would descend to the Weald near Clayton, drive their flocks along Lodge Lane, pass through the village of Keymer and then continue for the entire length of Ockley Lane to the point where Keymer Road and Junction Road now meet at the top of Station Hill.

The view gained was not the outlook we see today, but of a near desolate landscape sparsely dotted with clumps of gorse and one or two crudely constructed homesteads. The few buildings of substance were the farmhouse that stood where Queen's Crescent stands now and Hammonds Place. In the district called St. John's Common there were: a blacksmith's forge, the King's Head inn, a couple of cottages and little else. It was on the unenclosed Common, and then later in a field set aside for the purpose, that a livestock sale known as St. John's Sheep and Lamb Fair was held annually on 5th July.

This was the first Sheep and Lamb Fair of the year in Sussex and the interest generated was considerable. Flockmasters from places as far distant as Findon and Hastings were sure to attend, as were farmers, breeders, stockmen and other parties. In its hey-day, over 9,000 lambs, to say nothing of sheep, cattle and horses, were purchased and sold at the venue.

Like the seasons of the year and the arrival and departure of migrating birds, the Fair had always been, and always would be – at least that is what everyone thought. But of course nothing stays the same, and after the opening of the London to Brighton railway, the old ways began to change.

It was soon discovered that transporting sheep by train was more efficient and less expensive than trudging along highways and byways, while markets adjacent to the line were obviously better places to buy and sell than remote and difficult to get to commons.

The effect on St. John's was devastating: much of its business was taken over by cattle trading yards based alongside Hassocks, Haywards Heath and Lewes stations, and by the dawn of the 20th century the animals brought for sale had shrunk to a pitiful few.

Last minute attempts to re-kindle interest failed miserably, and by 1913, an institution that had existed since time immemorial, was consigned to the footnotes of history.

We are reminded of this because our stroll through the town starts at the very spot where the old time drovers caught their first glimpse of the place that became Burgess Hill. Nowadays it is a busy junction regulated by a roundabout; but in the Edwardian era, when motorised transportation was a rarity and the horse still King, a quaint looking triangular-shaped traffic island was all that was required to maintain orderly progress. It was surrounded by iron railings and contained within was a tiny patch of lawn, a lamp post and a couple of shrubs. Alongside stood a horse trough and a public drinking fountain, the last in the shape of a granite obelisk that was donated by a Mrs Piggott in memory of her husband.

The lady's thoughtful gesture was widely appreciated – except, that is, by a certain butcher, whose horse, despite its master's discordant bellowing, usually insisted on trotting round the reservation at least twice before proceeding on its way.

Directional signs attached to the island's gas lamp-standard indicated the whereabouts of the Congregational Church (now the United Reform Church) and the railway station. The church, with its pillars,

Fountain Corner
Where the butcher's pony and trap went round and round!

pilasters and Roman portico, was rather pompously described by the late John Betjeman as being the only example of worthwhile architecture in the town. His views on the railway station were not recorded.

No sign was necessary for Prospect Place, the head office and main retailing outlet of Hoadley's, a family-run departmental store with windows 'full of delights' that stretched round the corner into Junction Road. In addition to another smaller store in Lower Church Road, this hugely successful enterprise also had branches at Seaford and Ditchling, and for the sheer variety of goods on offer, it could match any similar establishment in the county. Frederick Hoadley, a native of Heathfield, founded the business in 1857 and it prospered almost immediately. His son and successor, James Hoadley, married Alice, the daughter of John Saxby, the inventor from Hassocks, who made his fortune by developing the railway point lock safety system. Saxby, for reasons that were never divulged, opposed the match. Bitter words were exchanged and for a short period the two families were at daggers drawn. However, true love eventually triumphed, the young couple were united and it would be nice to record that they all lived happily ever after.

Alas, it was not to be, for in the third generation, John Hoadley, son of James and the heir apparent, suddenly severed connections with his father's firm (again for reasons that were never disclosed) and worked instead for the Radio Relay company. At about the same time he married Eva, the youngest daughter of Edwin Street, the proprietor of the Victoria Pleasure Gardens. Their descendants live in the district to this day.

Prior to 1974, an imposing building constructed with red terracotta blocks cast a long shadow over the opposite side of the road. Called Wynnstay, it was erected around 1876 to serve as a dwelling for Mr Sampson Copestake, a wealthy industrialist and a great benefactor to the town. No history of the locality would be complete without a mention of his name, for it was largely due to him that St. Andrew's parochial district was created. According to 'The Story of Burgess Hill', written by A. H. Gregory, Mr Copestake gave £5,000 towards the endowment of the new parish; £1,000 for a temporary iron church; £1,000 towards the permanent church, and land of

Prospect Place
A view of Mr Hoadley's emporium in Junction Road. The rather grand building next door once housed the town's post office. The carriage in the centre of the picture was in all probability hired out by Mr George Miles, who styling himself a Jobmaster, had a business alongside the Burgess Hill Inn.

The Hoadley family (about 1935)
This photograph was taken in the garden of Mr James Hoadley's residence at 39 Church Road, Burgess Hill. James Hoadley is the white-haired gentleman seated at the centre. In the group are his son, John Hoadley (third in from the left), and his daughter-in-law, Eva Hoadley, née Street (second in from the left).

considerable value for the site, glebe and churchyard.

The original Wynnstay no longer exists, which is sad in a way, although it cannot be denied that the place was an architectural curiosity, its austere northern façade contrasting strangely with a southern aspect that more resembled a gingerbread house than the home of a hard-headed entrepreneur.

The views, however, were magnificent and stretched from Clayton windmills to Chanctonbury Ring. They, together with the health-inducing air and close proximity of the railway station, were undoubtedly one of the reasons why, after Mr Copestake moved on, the place was acquired by Professor Weidhaus, a gentleman of either Swiss or German extraction, who aimed to convert the premises into a nature cure establishment. In this capacity it became known as the Wynnstay Hydropathic Institution, or the Hydro for short. The enterprise remained a feature of the town until 1909, when, for various reasons, it was relocated to Franklands, a large property which overlooks the railway line approximately half a mile to the south of Burgess Hill.

In later years Wynnstay was the home of St. Joseph's Convent, a school for Catholic children who were taught by resident nuns, and at the time of writing there are still people in the district, including one of the authors of this book, who can recall the splendid parties that were held there every Christmas:

> … the normally strictly observed teacher/pupil relationship at the Convent was quite ignored on those happy occasions, and during games of hide-and-seek, when we had the virtual run of the building, the holy sisters kicked off their shoes and scampered round the corridors, laughing and squealing as much as their guests.

Wynnstay (about 1900)
A view of the southern aspect, when it was known as Wynnstay Hydro – the First English Nature Cure Establishment.

Wynnstay (about 1970)
A fine view of Sampson Copestake's old home; taken from the roof of Hoadley's departmental store just across the road.

Close by is one of the oldest taverns in the area, The Top House, or Burgess Hill Inn as it used to be called. Even further back, in the days when smugglers haunted the district, the place – or a building close to it – was known as The Anchor. It had a somewhat shady reputation.

There is little on record with regards to this, but if it could speak, the elderly oak by the steps that lead up to the bar entrance could surely tell a tale or two; it has been there long enough, as is proven by our photograph which is at least 100 years old and shows the tree looking much as it does now.

That it has survived is largely due to good luck and a non-prevailing wind, for in 1881, a fire swept through and completely gutted a large semi-detached building that stood a mere stone's throw away.

The cause, according to a newspaper at the time, was accidental, a faulty gas connection, and as there were no local emergency services to hand, a telegram was immediately transmitted to Brighton calling for assistance.

In the meanwhile, a supply of buckets was obtained from Hoadley's Stores, and a human chain linked up between a local pond and the scene of the blaze. By dint of hard labour the fire was practically extinguished when the Brighton fire engine eventually arrived, the matter was safely under control and what could have been saved, had been saved.

At one stage during the proceedings it was feared that a saddler's premises alongside would also go up in flames. It was decided, therefore, that his house and shop should be cleared without delay, and to quote from an original source,

> "No sooner were the doors opened than men rushed all over the premises clearing out everything, even to the fixtures and benches."

As a result, an anonymous contributor – someone who clearly had scant respect for the citizens of Burgess Hill – submitted a vitriolic description of the event to the Mid Sussex Times, and the editor, ignoring the near libellous content, published it. Part of the communication is reproduced here, penned under the name 'Fitzharry':

> It seemed as if there was hardly any life in the little town on a certain Saturday night, when a startling shout rent the air, "Fire! Fire!" With one start and one cry, Burgess Hill awoke. The cry was taken up from one end of the place to the other and emptied various public houses where the working men were investing their wages in beer. Close to Burgess Hill station – famed for its airiness and for the civility of its porters – a large house had taken fire, moreover, fanned by a gentle wind, it threatened the adjacent properties.
>
> It seemed as if every person in the place had gathered round the spot, and within quarter of an hour a little bit of hose had been procured, also a great number of buckets. Many endeavours were made to form lines to pass the buckets from a pond to the scene, but only a few people helped and they were not enough. In vain were great stalwart working men urged to lend a hand: not they! They flatly refused, they did not like to work without being paid. They delighted to stand idly in the road, jeering, laughing and joking, but would not exert themselves to help. Ah! then was the time to see the people of Burgess Hill, and to read their faces in the glare of the glowing fire.
>
> Meanwhile it threatened two other houses. One was a saddler's and it was decided to take things out of the shop. In rushed the mob, tore down everything that was nearest, and off they went. Some put their loads in safe places, others Heaven knows where; there are

Burgess Hill Inn
During the tenancy of Mr Thomas Lacey (a former chief inspector on the London, Brighton and South Coast Railway) the property, described as 'a pretty country inn' was extremely popular. The grounds were laid out for bowls, croquet and other amusements. During the summer months, teas and refreshments were available on the lawns, and good fishing was to be had from a large pond at the top end of the garden. A room at the back was used for meetings and various social gatherings, including regular First Aid classes held by a Dr Apthorp.

Station Hill

The garden wall of Tudor House (Lewis Slight's former residence) can be seen on the extreme left of this photograph. Just beyond is a turning (Green Lane) that leads to Franklands. To the right, renovated and repaired, are the properties that were damaged in the fire described by Fitzharry (page 8).

thieves, even in Burgess Hill. My heart bleeds for that man – for the unoffending saddler was the greatest sufferer of all. Then the Brigade arrived and the already half put out fire was finally extinguished. Honour the noble 20 men. The writer of this sketch can find good in anything. When the fire occurred Burgess Hill was dull and wanted waking up. Now the good people have something to talk about for the rest of their natural lives.

On the opposite side of the road, where a parade of shops and blocks of flats are nowadays situated, stood a fine old mansion called Tudor House, a place that warrants a mention if only because of a rather odd association with Brighton's high life back in the days when the Prince Regent ruled the social roost; a connection that was revealed in the West Sussex Gazette in April, 1869:

> One day this week a boy at Burgess Hill, who had been digging up the ground adjoining one of the villas there, came to his employer (a Brighton gentleman) with a little bit of bone or ivory in his hand, and holding it up, said, "See sir, what I have found." On inspection it proved to be about the last thing that anyone would have thought of picking up at Burgess Hill – it was the season ticket of Mrs Fitzherbert for the Italian opera house! The boy got something substantial for his find, which has since, we believe, become the property of Mr Smith Hannington.
>
> It may be asked how in the name of wonder did Mrs Fitzherbert's opera ticket come to Burgess Hill? The clue to the mystery is to be found, doubtless, in the fact that the late Mr Lewis Slight, the promoter of the Pavilion Purchase Act, resided at Burgess Hill, and was indeed the chief founder of that colony of Brighton.
>
> He was, we believe, in the habit of having refuse and the sweepings of the Pavilion brought to his place (Tudor House) for manure, and amongst the refuse of the Pavilion doubtless had lain for many a long year, the opera ticket.

For those who are unaware, Mrs Fitzherbert was a great favourite of the Prince Regent, and actually participated in some sort of marriage ceremony with him.

With regards to Mr Smith Hannington (the founder of Hanningtons of Brighton), we respectfully suggest that the newspaper account erred here, for that gentleman died in 1855, which was fourteen years before the opera ticket was discovered. However, his son, Mr Charles Smith Hannington was very much alive and living in nearby Hurstpierpoint, so it probably went to him. Mr Lewis Slight was responsible for building Tudor House, more commonly called 'Slight's Nest' because of its elevated position. He was a well-known Brighton Town Clerk and an astute businessman, which perhaps explains why, in certain circles, he was referred to as 'Loo Sly'.

Descend the hill to the town and it is striking how little the view has altered over the years. And with cabs parked on the forecourt and the wind whistling through the ticket office, the railway station also seems much the same, although the newspaper kiosk that fronts onto the road was originally located on the southbound platform. Of course there has been change; one would search in vain for the station master or porters, they went long ago. Now only a clerk remains to deal with the travelling public, and in his or her absence, a machine will issue a ticket! Indeed, the entire premises appears to be denuded of staff, a loudspeaker announces arrivals and departures, which is good enough in its way, but lacks the personal touch and is very different to the time when a local postman (a well-known eccentric by the name of Tony Shove), stood at the foot of the stairway and bawled out, "B—s Hill!" every time the mail train pulled in.

Station Hill
The gentleman in the dark suit on the right is George Chapman, husband of Lucy Chapman, owner of the Burgess Hill Steam Laundry in Royal George Road.

Burgess Hill Railway Station (about 1893)
Mr Jones, the Station Master.

Burgess Hill Railway Station (about 1893)
The proprietor of the news stand, which in those days, was situated on the southbound platform.

At the foot of Station Hill stands the Railway Hotel, formerly known as the Railway and Commercial Hotel. It was here in 1879 that it was agreed to adopt the Local Government Act and form a Local Board to look after the interests and welfare of Burgess Hill. This came about because of the number of unresolved complaints that had been made to the previous Authority (The Cuckfield Board of Guardians), about the insanitary state of the town. In particular were problems arising from cesspools, bad drains and the pollution of ditches – up until that time a number of houses in London Road were served by an open sewer.

The newly elected Board went to work with a will, and after borrowing the necessary money, built a sewage works on land at Bridge Farm and Freaks Farm, where, according to A. H. Gregory, Edwin Brown, a surveyor and sanitary inspector, conducted a profitable little sideline growing peppermint. The oil extracted from this plant supplemented his income by an additional £90 per annum.

On the western side of the Railway Hotel is the junction of Grove Road, which at one time led to a little hall known as the Union Chapel – where the local Congregationalists worshipped before the church in Junction Road was established.

Later it served as the Catholic church, and after St. Wilfrid's was erected in Station Road, the original building was retained as a church hall and youth club. In the latter capacity it was well attended with youngsters from the outlying district cycling to town on Sunday evenings to enjoy some social life and a rare opportunity to dance. A former member recalled the meetings with a great deal of pleasure.

"The evening always ended with the Hokee Cokee," she said. "It was a riotous affair, we all whirled round in a large circle singing and

Station Hill
The Railway and Commercial Hotel is to the extreme right of the picture, beyond which are the Bank Buildings. On the left, just past the two pedestrians, is the entrance to the station goods yard. On the far side of the junction are the grounds of Burgess Hill Farm.

shouting our heads off; everyone, even the priests, joined in. It was the greatest fun and left us absolutely breathless."

Later still the Jehovah's Witnesses acquired the lease and for several years it functioned as their Kingdom Hall. Then they too moved on, and in due course the small meeting house was demolished. The site has since been used as a car park.

Between the junctions of Grove Road and Mill Road stands a handsome terrace of shops known as the Bank Buildings. The name has no monetary connection but is derived from the fact that the premises were built on what had been a grassy bank fronting onto a meadow, where the first Captain of the Burgess Hill Fire Brigade, a Mr Tom Sinnock, used to auction cattle. Mr Sinnock held many public offices: Clerk to the Clayton and Keymer School Board; Clerk to the Ditchling Parish Council; Poor Law Guardian; Surveyor of the Highways, to name but a few. But he is probably best remembered as a cutting and vehement speaker at the Urban District Council debates. He and our grandfather, Edwin Street, had many clashes. On one occasion they conducted a mock fight in the chamber. On another, a discussion culminated in an almighty row, when our grandfather, (who, at six feet four inches and weighing 25 stones was the largest man in Mid Sussex), proposed widening a footpath in London Road. Mr Sinnock said it was perfectly adequate, it would take two normal-sized people with ease and should be just wide enough for Mr Street.

Opposite to the hotel, a road leads to the old railway goods yard, an area that now houses a builder's merchant's warehouse and a garage business. Back in 1906 it was to be the scene of yet another disastrous fire at Burgess Hill, one that originated at a pumping house situated within the compound.

The 'vehement speaker'
Mr Thomas Sinnock, in his fire brigade uniform. The initials on the helmet, B.H. & M.S.F.B. stand for 'Burgess Hill and Mid Sussex Fire Brigade'.

The photograph, taken shortly before his death in August 1914, bears the inscription "With Tom's love" which is in pleasant contrast to some of the more peppery remarks he is reputed to have made.

By some incredible mishap, containers of combustible liquids stored inside the building, ignited. This was followed by a series of tremendous explosions, flames shot high into the air and a burning river of oil threatened to engulf a reservoir holding a further 40,000 gallons.

The local Fire Brigade, together with crews from Hassocks, Hurstpierpoint and Brighton, raced to the scene and fought the blaze with great effect, thus managing to avert any further catastrophe. As a result of their efforts, the reservoir was saved, but buildings and equipment of considerable value were destroyed, with – according to a witness – a number of splendid oak trees that bordered the property, "going up like Roman candles!"

Continuing in a frivolous vein, the goods yard featured in an article that appeared in the Mid Sussex Times during 1911. Under the heading, 'Bullock Evades Pursuers' it stated:

> At the beginning of last week, a bullock belonging to a local butcher, arrived at the goods yard at Burgess Hill. It was getting dark, the invigorating air of the 'Health Resort' made him frisky and off he bolted down the railway track. Railway men, butchers and others went in pursuit, as a policeman would say, but the animal was lost to view.
>
> Till midnight he was hunted for, but in vain.
>
> When the sun rose next morning, he was found staring and wagging his tail near Frankland's Bridge, and was driven off in triumph.
>
> He will not play such tricks again.

Burgess Hill Farmhouse
The farmhouse was one of the oldest dwellings in the district, probably pre-dating all but Hammonds Place. There has been much conjecture about its history, but none that is worth repeating. Little is really known, nor is it likely to be, because, in an act of official vandalism, the property was pulled down in the period following the end of the Second World War.
This photograph was taken immediately before demolition, when everything worthwhile had already been removed.

The Farmhouse which stood more or less adjacent to the goods yard, was demolished in the 1950s. It was an ancient building with a huge chimney stack and some fine woodwork that dated from Tudor times. In the past, hops had been grown on the land, and it was one of three farms in the district to be owned by our grandfather, Edwin Street. He divided the property into separate tenements, and in due course his second son, Frederick, took up residence in one of these with his newly married wife, the former Miss Ada Whall.

Burgess Hill Farmhouse yard (circa 1880)
A view of the area just west of the farmhouse. Buildings in Station Road can be seen through the trees. The photographer, Simeon Norman, was the managing director of Norman and Burt Ltd., the well-known firm of church and ecclesiastical builders.

Her niece, Mrs Ruby Cook, referred to the premises in a letter that was published in 'About Town', the magazine produced by Burgess Hill Town Council. Stating that the place dated from the 13th century, she went on to say:

> I actually slept there as my uncle and aunt lived there. It belonged to the Street family, my aunt having married Mr Fred Street.
>
> Going to bed was a real adventure, trying to climb what was really a ladder balancing a candle with one hand, and holding onto a rope on the wall as a hand rail. Having arrived at the top, you would emerge through a hole in the floor and enter one large room divided by a green curtain. Auntie and uncle slept one side of the curtain, and my sister and I on the other.
>
> Rats could be heard running in the roof. Foxes roamed the garden and could be heard barking. My uncle kept chickens, so when he went to the lavatory which was outside the house, he always took his gun with him. Sitting there one night with his gun at the ready, a fox decided to have poultry for supper. Uncle shot it, and had its skin made into a fox fur for auntie.

On the hairpin bend opposite to the Farmhouse – where Station Road and Church Road meet – stood the Brighton Union Bank and immediately in front of that grew the Gospel Tree, or as some people called it, the Reformers Tree. The spot was much frequented, a place like Hyde Park Corner, where people were free to express their views, and according to Ivy Dudeney, "… there were always plenty of them." As a girl during the early years of the 20th century, she had been a boarding pupil at the nearby Elmhurst School for Young Ladies, and could recall occasions when the meetings were so unruly, and the hecklers so vociferous, that a policeman was required to keep the peace.

She said that a crowd also assembled there on Sunday afternoons, not to make trouble, but to listen to the Salvation Army Band, which, having marched down Station Hill from Hoadley's Corner, formed up beneath the tree and played hymn music for half an hour or so. Then, after preaching the word, the bandsmen, accompanied by the rattle of collection boxes and the muffled beat of a drum, returned to their citadel in Cyprus Road.

Today it would hardly be advisable for large numbers of people to assemble outside the bank, because the locality is one of the busiest junctions in Burgess Hill and close to the heart of the main trading centre. Both sides of Upper Church Road are now lined with shops, offices and other buildings, while in Station Road, businesses lead down from the hill and round the corner into Queen's Crescent. This later development, which screened the Farmhouse from general view, began in 1933 and at the same time the road and pavement were set back to make the crossroads less dangerous for traffic.

The idea of improving the area's facilities was hardly new, indeed it had been in existence since the beginning of the 20th century when the town was still being promoted as a health resort, and with this in mind an urban councillor, Henry Burt, went so far as to prepare plans for a 'beauty spot' square between Bank Buildings and the Farmhouse in order to improve the entrance to the district from the railway station. But this and another scheme for the construction of an entirely new thoroughfare intended to link Mill Road with Junction Road was eventually abandoned.

It was in 1900 or thereabouts that the name of the Brighton Union Bank, an establishment that was open for business only on Tuesdays and Fridays between the hours of 10.30 am and 4 pm, was altered to Barclays. The new manager, Mr C. H. Winterbottom, a recent arrival

The Gospel Tree
The Brighton Union Bank is all but concealed by the Gospel Tree (also called the Reformers Tree), around which hundreds of religious, political and other gatherings were held. An attempt to stop the practice which caused congestion at the crossroads, met with little success, and it required nature to do the trick. That occurred in 1933, when the tree was blown down by a gale. Nobody was hurt, but, according to the Mid Sussex Times: "…two women close by received a shock."

in the vicinity, would probably have altered his name as well, had he been aware of the amusement it provided for the more coarsely inclined members of the local public!

The first buildings on the bank side of Station Road included the Reading Room, or Hall, erected in 1893 at the expense of Mr W. Stevens of Broadhill. It was described as a public house without alcoholic drink, or in other words, a free reading and recreation room conducted on temperance principles. The building boasted a coffee bar and two public rooms, one of which was capable of seating about 100 people. In 1922 it became the Burgess Hill Red Triangle Club, a Y.M.C.A. organisation for youth, and in later years the premises served several other local organisations, including the Red Cross. It is with us still, in the guise of a restaurant.

Next to the hall stood a substantial three-storeyed building; the former Elmhurst School referred to earlier, which in later years became the local Ministry of Labour Employment Exchange, managed by a Mr Mycock. There was a suggestion at the end of the Second World War that the property should be converted into a post office – the main sorting office was already situated at the rear – but the idea did not obtain Government approval, despite the fact that the residential part of the building was occupied by the Postmaster. The decision instead was that this fine property should be demolished, and in its place a new 'matchbox' shaped Post Office would be erected to serve the town. In the meantime, the Ministry of Labour office was housed in the old telephone exchange in Mill Road.

The area at the junction of Mill Road and Upper Church Road was once known as Terry's Corner, the site of the business premises of Edward Terry and Son, whose company sold about every commodity imaginable. It was founded by Edward Boys Terry back in the days when lighting was obtained by gas or oil lamps, indeed, the days of rushlights and horn lanterns were not long past. But none of this would do for Mr Terry, old world charms had their place, but he was a go-ahead man, and so with the aid of his scientifically minded son, Horace, he constructed an electricity generating plant in stables at the rear of 6 Church Road. The result was that when the lights were switched on, the brilliance of Terry's Corner became the talk of the town, and set a standard to which all aspired.

The Gospel Tree
In July 1913, suffragists from all over the country marched to London to demonstrate the strength of their unity, and to enable the woman's voice to be heard where it mattered. Groups set out from every town in England, their numbers increasing as they marched along, and rallies were held on the way. This photograph shows one such – beneath the Gospel Tree at Burgess Hill. A note on the back of the picture informs us that the policeman on duty was PC Foord.

The Gospel Tree
The photograph taken from the Brighton Union Bank shows the Salvation Army Band playing beneath the Gospel Tree. Referring to this practice, a correspondent in the Burgess Hill 'About Town' magazine, recalled that on Sunday afternoons, the Salvationists would first play at Hoadley's Corner, and then march quietly off until passing the Burgess Hill Inn; "at this point they burst forth into loud and challenging music".

Station Hill – Edward VII Coronation
The citizens of Burgess Hill always enjoyed dressing up and having parades. The town might have been designed for the purpose. All organisations and groups participated, and after they had assembled in the area round Hoadley's, they went down Station Hill in an orderly procession, making, as can be seen from this photograph, a magnificent spectacle. From that point on, Church Road was lined by cheering crowds as the column made its way to St. John's Park, where all concerned were addressed by local dignitaries and congratulated for their enthusiasm and turn-out. Then, more often than not, they went to the Victoria Pleasure Gardens and spent the rest of the day in sport, feasting and entertainment.

A view from Terry's Corner
During the closing years of its existence, St. John's Sheep and Lamb Fair was held in a field next to the Victoria Pleasure Gardens (now a factory estate) and finally, in a meadow alongside Station Road. The sheep in this photograph could have been going to either venue, it is hard to say. However, we are fairly sure that they arrived by train.

Church Road looking east (about 1905)
The first police station in Burgess Hill is to the left of this photograph, and the Local Board Office stood alongside.
A tunnel or enclosed passageway between the buildings led to the town's original fire station.

At this stage of the journey we are hoping that our stroll through the town will be a comfortable exercise for the reader, and very different to that experienced by Fitzharry, who in yet another of his bilious communications to the Mid Sussex Times in 1881, described the route as follows:

> … let us go from the station to the church. We pass a lot of newly erected shops. I saw those shops built and know all about them! It is a very pleasant road from the station to the church, indeed, it is considered to be the finest in the whole place. Along this road to the church is a splendid pathway, just allowing two persons to walk comfortably abreast. On either side of you is a magnificent view of workmen digging clay! On the outside of the pathway usually runs a lot of water; perhaps the day will come when Burgess Hill will be provided with a river, it is said to possess a floating population! It is only when Burgess Hill is in the height of its glory that I understand what this expression means!

Acerbic as they are, Fitzharry's comments provide us with a tiny glimpse of the district as it once was. Nowadays as we look westwards from Terry's Corner, a very different scene greets the eye. Although many of the old buildings are still in use, the pavements are broad enough, water drains away as it should, and while workmen still dig holes more frequently than we might wish, it is to improve our services, not to search for clay.

Modern offices and shops – including branches of well known multiple stores – with flats above, now dominate the area. They extend along Upper Church Road and the length of Church Walk, having replaced earlier properties such as Redlands, Dudley Terrace, and Latchetts (Simeon Norman's lovely old home). Also gone is the Baptist Chapel where Ephraim Standing preached for 49 years, and Aspendell, where he lived.

One-time neighbours in the area were the Urban District Council and Lloyds Bank. They shared the former Constitutional Club building, which, built by a local man, William Oram, was officially opened with a fanfare of trumpets by Viscount Cranbrook in 1892. It was a social and political club which leaned towards the Conservative and Unionist party, but the aspirations of the founders were not realised and five years later the premises was placed onto the market. The Urban District Council, whose somewhat pokey offices were then adjacent to the town's police station, showed interest, only to have their proposal rejected by a meeting of ratepayers. Other suggestions also received the thumbs down, and in due course the P.N.E.U. School took over the property.

By 1928 the Council was becoming quite desperate for space, and so when Wynnstay was put up for sale, it seemed to be the answer to their prayers. They immediately applied for sanction to borrow £3,750 which would cover cost and improvements, but were again met with strong opposition. This included a petition bearing 279 voluntary signatures "from every class of inhabitant and rate-payer." The Council then looked to the Ministry for support – it was not forthcoming. That body felt that a stop-gap solution of alterations and additions to the existing offices would supply sufficient accommodation to meet their requirements. Frustrated at this response, the Chairman and Clerk travelled up to Whitehall to discuss the matter further, but in vain. After much debate nothing was finalised and the matter was placed into abeyance.

That these were difficult times for the Council is beyond dispute. Only four years earlier 10 of the 12 elected members had resigned en masse regarding a question relating to footpaths. Now their detractors, having tasted blood were at them again, as may be

Church Road (about 1914)
This is Mr Bert Killick outside Redlands, a private residence that stood on the site now occupied by W.H. Smith. Mr Killick is believed to have been the first person to hold a Hackney Carriage licence for a motor vehicle in Burgess Hill. He was an excellent driver and mechanic, and drove staff cars for senior military personnel during the First World War. In later years he ran a coal business in Junction Road.

Church Road looking west (about 1922)
In this photograph, what nowadays is the entrance to one of the town's central car parks, is enclosed by a white gate – an obstacle that had to be removed when the area beyond became the site of Burgess Hill's second fire station.
In those days firemen were summoned to duty by an ex-World War Two air raid siren, and by the time the first man arrived, Church Road was crowded with children waiting to see the big red fire engine, bells ringing and tyres squealing, come roaring round the corner.
Lloyds Bank's association with the town goes back to 1875, when the then Hampshire Bank opened a sub-branch at Hoadley's stores, appointing Frederick Hoadley as Agent. Two years later it amalgamated to form the Hampshire and North Wilts Banking Company, and in 1878, changed its name to the Capital and Counties Bank. In 1915 it moved to Church Road Chambers (the old Constitutional Club) and has remained there ever since. The merger of Lloyds and Capital took place in 1918.

gathered by some of the heated correspondence that was appearing in the local press. In fact it was probably the general discord that prompted the highly respected Vicar of St. Andrew's, the Reverend Gerald Tindall Atkinson, to write a ditty entitled 'Surprises' and to submit it for publication in the Mid Sussex Times, two verses from which are reproduced here:

> We are living today in the queerest of towns,
> For up to the station is past Mr Down's,
> When Keymer Road's down it has to come up,
> And it fills to the brim the poor rate-payer's cup.
> For it's up, up, up, the rates go.
> We're down on our uppers; our fortunes are low,
> When the Council thus rates us, the workhouse awaits us,
> And it's down, down, downwards we go.
>
> Some Councils are homes of blissful repose,
> Where nobody treads on the neighbouring toes.
> We always imagine they sat down to meet,
> Produced food for thought without friction or heat.
> But some rise, rise, rise to their feet.
> Their spirit is fiery, they serve it out neat.
> They soon must grow thinner, with din for their dinner,
> When it's rise, rise, rise to their feet.

(Note: Mr Down ran a licensed victualler's premises on the corner of Church Road and Cyprus Road.)

In due course the U.D.C. realised its ambitions, not by acquiring Wynnstay, but by moving into its original choice, the old Constitutional Club, where it remained for many years serving the people of Burgess Hill. However, for one reason or another it was unable to shake off a reputation for self-interest, suspicions of which

Church Road looking east
Behind the railed fence to the left of the photograph were the offices of Maynard and James (solicitors in law). The late Lieutenant-Colonel S. T. Maynard T.D., J.P., was in his day, an influential man in the district, and a former Commandant of the Kent and Sussex Cyclist Brigade.

The building on the eastern corner of Cyprus Road belonged to Mr Down, the licensed victualler whose name appears on the previous page. On the opposite side of the road (where the pedestrian is standing) a footpath passed through a brick field to the late Clifton Road, a pretty residential thoroughfare, which before it was demolished and buried in concrete, led to Station Road.

Church Road looking west (circa 1905)
This well-known photograph shows how much an area can change, yet still be recognisable. Latchetts, Simeon Henry Norman's home (on the left) stood where a parade of shops stand now, while the land to the north was virtually undeveloped.

were raised yet again, when on a certain date in 1953, passers-by were startled to see one of their elected members being physically ejected from the Chambers by an officer of the law and then marched up to the police station where he was charged with abusive and disorderly behaviour.

The accused man's name was John Charles Bee-Mason, or the 'Stinger' as he was popularly known, an independent councillor, who, while enjoying strong support from the town's voters, had earned the implacable enmity of his colleagues. That day was a sad one for local government, a day when small town scandal became the subject of national headlines in the columns of the Daily Telegraph and Morning Post, no less.

The Daily Telegraph and Morning Post – 22nd April, 1953

COUNCILLOR, 78, DEFIES COURT

"I'm ready to go to gaol"

Disputes within the Burgess Hill, Sussex, Urban Council led yesterday to Court proceedings. Mr John Charles Bee-Mason, 78, of Junction Road, Burgess Hill, a member, was fined £1 on each of two summonses, with two guineas costs.

He was also ordered to enter into recognisance of £50 within seven days to be of good behaviour for a year. He refused to pay the fines or to enter into the recognisance and said he was prepared to go to gaol.

Mr Bee-Mason is a bee-keeper and a former Arctic explorer. He is an Independent member of the Council. The summonses heard at Haywards Heath Magistrates Court, alleged abusive and disorderly behaviour within the Council Chamber.

Mr Peter Harrison, prosecuting, said that at a monthly meeting of the Council on 2nd April, Bee-Mason requested that a certain item on the minutes be read, as he wished to speak on it. The Chairman, Squadron Leader Page, ruled that the matter was private and did not concern the Council.

ONE OF THE BIGGEST SCANDALS

A dispute followed in which the defendent produced a block of wood and banged it repeatedly on the table. Finally a police officer was summoned and Bee-Mason left the Chamber with the remark, "Goodnight, monkeys".

Bee-Mason in Court said the Chairman had lied when he said that the item on the minutes was a private one. It referred to one of the 'biggest scandals in the history of housing in Burgess Hill'. Two officials and four Councillors will be subpoenaed in connection with a Court action pending.

"If an elected representative of the Council can't speak on an item on the minutes without being arrested he might as well live in Moscow," he said. He declared that at previous Council meetings he had been the victim of 'disorderly conduct' by other Councillors whenever he spoke. "I didn't squeal for the police."

"I am pleading for the poor and needy. I object to the Councillors' friends with money getting Council houses. I am ready to go to gaol even if it is only to expose the treatment that invalids, widows and orphans have received at the hands of the Burgess Hill Council."

Bee-Mason was a formidable and complex character who combined the qualities of a 'Boy's Own' hero with the views of a zealot. So before acquainting ourselves with the outcome of the Court proceedings, some information concerning the man's background might be of interest.

Perhaps best described as an old fashioned adventurer, he had been a member of Shackleton's 'Quest' Expedition, 1921; the Oxford University Arctic Expedition in 1924; the British Arctic Expedition in 1925 and the Bolivian 'Green Hell' Expedition, 1928. To all of which he was the official photographer.

It is an odd fact that one of the most successful beehives to be used in Mid Sussex, was designed by Bee-Mason while the explorers' ship, *The Island,* was frozen in the Polar pack ice off Franz Joseph Land. Based on the lines of a Swiss bee house, he had a model constructed on his return to England, and after tests were made, discovered that it yielded twice as much honey as one of his regular hives, and – a point of considerable importance – the bees did not swarm. In addition to these advantages, the little creatures were more thoroughly insulated from temperature change, and it was possible to get at the brood nest with less disturbance.

Bee-Mason was a great advocate of the benefits of honey. At the outbreak of the Second World War, he ran an advertising campaign throughout the country in which he urged beekeepers to donate a percentage of their product to the armed forces, especially sub-mariners. So successful was the project that the sheer amount left at dockyard gates probably created more problems than it solved, and in an official acknowledgement of the gift, a spokesman for the Admiralty added a heartfelt rider: "The officers and men thank you all for your incredible generosity. We now have enough honey to last for the foreseeable future. Please, please – send no more."

During the General Strike of 1926, Bee-Mason offered his services to Southern Rail. He was eminently qualified to do so, being willing and able to drive an engine, act as a guard, signal man, porter, or indeed, do anything, go anywhere.

The Authorities placed him in charge of the signal box at Portslade Station, and, early one morning whilst approaching the premises, he found his way barred by three strikers. Their leader, whom he later described as a 'big brute of a man' offered him violence if he entered railway property. It was an action he would regret for Bee-Mason struck out, catching the thug full in the face with his fist. The three men then rushed at him, but Bee-Mason, drawing out a knife with a ten inch blade (normally used for skinning seals), warned them to keep off or he would use it!

The same evening, a police inspector called at the signal box and informed him that the Strike Committee had complained that he had assaulted one of their pickets and then threatened them with an offensive weapon. As a result he understood that a group of strikers intended to rush the box in a body and exact their revenge. But Bee-Mason was unperturbed, knowing they could only mount the steps two at a time, he felt sure that he could handle them, and so continued to perform his duty. That, he stated, was the best answer he could give to those who asked how he could call himself an Englishman.

After a lifetime of adventure and achievement, for which he was awarded the MBE, Bee-Mason settled down to retirement in Burgess Hill, first at Queensmead, Folders Lane, and later in Junction Road. However, it proved to be anything but peaceful, as controversy of one sort or another seemed to accompany him wherever he went.

For instance, a neighbour's wife complained of his practice of keeping a large dog chained up in the garden, "all day and all night the poor beast". His response was that the animal didn't suffer at all, and, anyway, it was none of her business.

"Then I will make it my business," she retorted, and promptly informed the R.S.P.C.A. When inspectors from the organisation arrived to investigate, they discovered that the dog was there alright, but it failed to bark as they approached; nor yet wagged its tail. It did nothing at all – it was made of stone!

This, then, was the man who appeared at Court on 21st April, 1953, to answer criminal charges. After pleading guilty he told the presiding magistrates that, as an elected member of the Burgess Hill Urban District Council, he had the right to comment upon any item on the minutes, something that had been denied him. If prevented from doing so at the next meeting, he would hammer the table again.

When informed that he would be bound over to keep the peace for 12 months and fined £2 and costs, he refused to be bound over or to pay one farthing. Upon being told that he had seven days to think it over, he responded, "I don't want seven minutes; you have my answer."

The following week he was sentenced to two months' imprisonment.

Bee-Mason served his time at Brixton where he made tabs for mail bags. "I was amongst some of the worst criminals. I sat at a table with four other men. One was there for assault with violence, another for robbery, a third for criminal assault on a boy, and the fourth for indecent behaviour towards a little girl. What was my crime? I had claimed the right of free speech, had hit a table with a piece of wood, and, because I refused to promise not to repeat it under similar circumstances, I was thrown into prison amongst criminals."

He was released from custody on Saturday, 6th June, 1953.

Two days later the news was reported in the Daily Mail:

HOME FROM GAOL TO VILLAGE CHEERS

'Councillor Rivals Parade'

The villagers were holding their Coronation carnival procession when 78-year-old Councillor John Bee-Mason came home from gaol this weekend to Burgess Hill, Sussex. And their cheers for him were even louder than those for the tableaux.

His bungalow in Junction Road was draped with large 'Welcome Home' posters.

He had a job to open his front door, for hundreds of letters from sympathisers and admirers from all over the country were piled on the mat. There were presents, too, including an iced cake.

Until late last night he was kept busy opening the door to callers, waving to well-wishers who cheered him from the road, and answering the phone.

'Fight Goes On'

Of his spell in prison, he said yesterday: "It was not exactly pleasant. I was treated exactly the same as any other prisoner, but I did sense an atmosphere of sympathy."

And of the future: "I haven't given up my fight against those on the Council who would like to silence me. I shall not be at the next Council meeting on Thursday – I shall be in London talking over the next move with a famous Q.C."

The advice he would appear to have received was that any future allegations of misconduct were best made outside the Chamber, not in.

And so it came about. At forthcoming Council assemblies, Bee-Mason was a virtually silent participant. His bark had gone, but not his bite. That was reserved for public meetings entitled, 'Why I Went to Prison'. He even wrote a book on the subject; copies still turn up from time to time, and while the contents might seem a trifle naive (the man was a dedicated Spiritualist), there is no questioning his integrity, or the fact that he brought a sparkle to local electioneering:

> You've sampled the Council duds galore,
> The monkey brigade aren't fighters;
> So give Bee-Mason your vote once more,
> And let him sting the blighters.

Those who took part in this small town drama have long since passed away, their names mostly forgotten, which is just as well; for regardless as to the rights and wrongs of the situation, we are left with a memory of harsh words and poorly judged actions resulting in the occurence of one of the most shameful episodes in the history of local government at Burgess Hill.

A short distance from the former Council Chambers stands the parish church of St. John the Evangelist, the erection of which commenced in 1861, and the consecration by the Bishop of Chichester (Dr Gilbert) taking place just two years later. Then in 1865, by an order in Council, 'The District Chapelry of St. John the Evangelist in the County of Sussex' was formed as the result of an application to the Ecclesiastical Commissioners.

The church is a handsome red brick construction in the Early Decorated style, and stands in a slightly elevated position on land that once formed part of a holding known as Hillmans Farm.

Crescent Road at its junction with Church Road (about 1960)
At first glance this view is not easy to recognise. In fact the photograph was taken from Crescent Road and looks in a south-westerly direction. On the immediate left, the lamp marks the boundary of the war memorial. The turning beyond is Church Road (now Church Walk) which runs east through the town to the railway station. On the right one can just make out the graveyard wall.
The villas that we see, stood on the southern side of the road as it curved its way round St. John's Church. They have since been demolished to make room for Civic Way.

Whether they are aware of it or not, many people who were born and bred in or around Burgess Hill, have a recorded link with the area. This is because number 53 Church Road, one of the two buildings featured in the picture, was the Lancelot Studio. The proprietor, Mr W. L. Elkington, who ran the business in the 1930s and 1940s, was a specialist in child portraiture and probably photographed most of the town's youngsters during his time there. (The property next door was used as a dental surgery.)

Outside of St. John's Church

In this wintery but pleasant scene outside the parish church, the roof-top silhouetted behind the coachman's head is that of Freshfield House, the former home of the Meeds family.

On St. Luke's Day, 18th October, 1901, the premises ceased to be a private residence and were officially opened as a place to bring up boys as 'sober, honest, God-fearing citizens'. Known henceforth as 'St. Luke's Home for Waifs and Strays' it became an Incorporated Society run under the auspices of the Church of England.

To discover what the boys thought of the establishment has proved to be difficult, for they are scattered throughout the country, if not the world. It seems that upon leaving, the majority of them enlisted into the armed forces, the merchant service, or went to work on farms in the various Dominions.

However, we did trace one, a gentle, quietly spoken man of retirement age, and his response to our request for recollections was entirely unexpected.

"Yes, I remember the *** place," he retorted. "If only I could forget. If I had ever had any photographs I would have torn them up!"

Church of St. John the Evangelist (about 1865)
This surely is one of the earliest photographs of St. John's Church ever to be published. As can be seen by the rustic fence surrounding the graveyard, work on the project is not yet completed.
Church Road is little more than a rutted cart track and barely recognisable, while Crescent Road doesn't exist.

The western tower is surmounted by a spire containing both a clock and chimes (eight bells). Amongst the memorials that may be found within, are several to the Crunden's, once one of the prominent families in Burgess Hill. In particular, Mr Frederick Crunden, who was a generous supporter of parochial activities. He was instrumental in beautifying the interior of the building, and in 1907, presented a site in Park Road for the establishment of the Vicarage. He also donated a substantial amount to the building fund.

The organ, which cost over £800, was a gift from Dr Withers Moore, J.P., in remembrance of his wife. Windows commemorating the doctor himself, were given by his family.

A fine oak pulpit was placed in the church as a public tribute to the late Simeon Norman (an important figure in the town) and a matching lectern is a family memorial of Mr and Mrs James Meeds.

It should also be acknowledged that Colonel Elwood of Clayton Priory (a soldier who distinguished himself in the Indian Campaigns) gave £500 towards the cost of the newer northern aisle.

The clock, purchased by public subscription, was inserted into the spire in honour of Queen Victoria's Golden Jubilee in 1887. The chimes, also purchased by public subscription, were installed 10 years later to commemorate her Diamond Jubilee.

Two more bells were added in 1900 and the remaining three were hung in 1904.

The registers date from 1863.

The view from the steeple (about 1968)
This photograph, taken at the beginning of the town centre development project, presents an aspect that few would recognise now. Instead of containing police station, fire station, office blocks and school, the somewhat desolate landscape once known as the 'Rye Rumps' and 'Brow', all that remained of one of the great 'tile and pipe' manufacturing areas of Burgess Hill, was virtually empty. Thomas Holman's bakery (the premises peeping through the lime trees) was a long-established business, and the proprietor's parents, who were married before the church was built, walked to Clayton each Sunday for worship. This was the accepted practice then. People walked to Communion, came home for breakfast, only to return once more for mid-morning service. To have journeyed there and back twice before mid-day must have been a daunting task, even for the fittest parishioner, especially when bearing in mind the dreadful condition of the roads. Therefore one wonders what Mrs Holman was thinking of, when, after St. John's was opened, she was heard to observe, "We shall shall miss our walk to Clayton".

A splendid view of the surrounding district may be obtained from the vicinity of the spire, but, hardly surprisingly, access to such a vantage point rarely occurs. However, maintenance work in 1908 provided some bold spirits with the chance, according to a brief report in the Mid Sussex Times:

> … the boys of Burgess Hill have lofty ideas. That is apparent by the fact that they have been climbing some considerable distance up ladders placed against the tower by steeplejacks. A plank was positioned against the lowest ladder to prevent the lads from going up, but they ascended on the other side. They have since had the 'rise taken out of them' – by the cane.

Following the road round the church, we come to St. John's Park, the main open-air recreational area in Burgess Hill, a place about which Fitzharry, in his final contribution to these pages, had this to say:

> … we go past the Church, enter a better, or worse road, whichever you like, and see a queer looking building. "What on earth is that place?" we ask a labourer. "Don't know thoart place? Why, that's the Institute"*, is the answer. Yes, that's the Institute, where the Local Board meet, and the local bored talk over their complaints; where concerts and entertainments of every description are given. Where young ladies, husband fishing are taught design, and all the gossip of the place is talked over.
>
> But we must leave the Institute to notice the Park. This beautiful resort in all weathers is the glory of Burgess Hill. It consists of an uneven piece of meadow guarded with some broken wire fences and possesses a few young trees. Certain butchers in the neighbourhood make it a pasture for their flocks.

(*The Institute, now known as the Park Centre, was used by the Local Board before they moved into the offices next to the police station.)

Fitzharry was at least right about the butchers – as previously indicated, our grandfather was one. It is on record that, in 1893, Edwin Street hired the feed of St. John's Park from the Local Board, as a yearly tenant at £6 per annum, an arrangement that he relinquished (to avoid allegations of conflicting interests), when he was elected to the Council. His shop was situated on the south-eastern corner of the crossroads, and the slaughter house was positioned a little further up Lower Church Road, which made it conveniently close to the meadow in question.

On being led from the field, the poor creatures were well aware of the fate that awaited them, and often attempted to escape.

On one such occasion, a 40-stone sow, having eluded her would-be captors, discovered all that stood between her and freedom was a butcher's assistant by the name of Teddy Alwen.

"Stop her Teddy," roared our grandfather.

Teddy bravely grabbed at the animal's huge ears, but, squealing with fright, the pig ducked her head between the young fellow's legs and ran off up London Road with him on her back!

In later years the grazing tenancy was acquired by Mr David William Rainy, a retired farmer from Somerset who liked to keep a small number of cows as a hobby. He died in 1928 and his daughter, the late Miss Alice Rainy of Newport Road, enjoyed reminiscing about 'the good old days' when she helped her father with the milking.

The story of St. John's Park as a place of recreation goes back to 1871 when a society was formed at Burgess Hill to provide working men with reading rooms and the opportunity to participate in social activities, to which end a house was rented in Church Road.

Holman's Bakery

This oddly assorted group gathered outside the premises, appear to be receiving goods through the window. Why we are not sure. They include Mr Tom Allfrey (third in from the left), and Mrs Elkington, (the lady in the spotted dress) whose husband was the proprietor of the nearby Lancelot Studio.

St. John's Road

Mr George Whiting of Fowels Farm, Royal George Road, is here seen driving his milk float past 'Hiawatha' (since demolished), the curiously-named home of Mr Albert Edward Chapman, one-time organist and music teacher at St. John's Church.

Mr Chapman could hardly have resided closer to his place of employment, and it is an odd coincidence that in more recent times, another church organist lived equally near to St. John's. He was Mr John Glandfield of 'Kentwyns' (also demolished), which stood on the present site of Warner Court in Crescent Road.

St. John's Church Choir (about 1900)
The Reverend John Le Mare Shallis, the Vicar of St. John's, is seated in the centre of the group.
His ministry, which lasted nearly 20 years, will be remembered not only as a period of church extension in the parish, but also one of intensive beautifying of the Parish Church itself. It was during his incumbency that the first stained glass windows (in memory of Dr James Braid) were installed, and the building of the north aisle and the new clergy and choir vestry commenced. With reference to Dr Braid; he was the physician who, in 1876, amputated P. C. Charles Tester's thumb at Burgess Hill Police Station. It had been bitten by a Thomas Weller of Ditchling during the course of a drunken brawl, and the wound, which became infected, failed to heal, thereby posing a serious threat to the officer's health. As it was, he eventually returned to light duties.

St. John's Church, western aspect (about 1865)
Another historic view of the church, and one that confirms the remoteness of the location. The only other building to be seen (just) is the cottage to the left of the picture. It stands there still and can be found in Crescent Road. The corner in the foreground was as hazardous for vehicles then as it is now, for gleaning through old newspaper cuttings, we discovered that Percy Jones, a delivery boy employed by Thomas Holman, crashed his bicycle three times on the same day whilst attempting to negotiate the bend.

A cricket club was formed for the society's members and the President (a General Hall) allowed them to play on the land which now forms part of the park.

Following his death, a great friend by the name of Madame Emily Temple, decided to erect St. John's Institute to his memory, and then presented it to the town. She also bequeathed six and a half acres of land for a public park and appointed three trustees to be responsible for its welfare. Furthermore, she ordered that money realised from the sale of her furniture should be paid to the trustees and be invested for the maintenance of the Institute and land. This came about, and on the death of the trustees, the whole thing was formed into a local charity scheme under the auspices of the Charity Commissioners.

In 1891 the park was taken over by the Local Board, which promptly spent £300 in levelling and fencing it. Later it passed to the Burgess Hill Urban District Council, and readers might guess that when that body proposed spending £650 on the erection of a pavilion, and a further £100 on extending the pitch, there was an uproar in the Chamber and the suggestion was rejected.

But the Authorities bided their time, and during the difficult years between the two world wars, were able to provide considerable employment for local people by extending the park on its western side. In addition, improvements to the entire area were effected by the construction of both hard and grass surfaced tennis courts, pathways, flower beds, a miniature golf course and a boating-cum-paddling pool. Later on a swimming pool was added to the attractions, making the area an extremely popular venue during the summer months.

From the London Road, Burgess Hill, Sussex.

St John's Park
This view from Park Road shows the area, complete with livestock, whilst it was still a meadow. A blacksmith's forge stood at the London Road end, which is where Mr W. S. Dale and his sons, Charles, Alfred, William and Ebenezer, craftsmen every one, worked for many years. Who recalls them now, or remembers the ring of the anvil; the smell of burning as horses' hooves were shod? They are memories of a bygone age. Likewise, what remains of Dale Villa, or the Chestnut tree that cast its shadow across the road? Nothing, yet they once figured prominently in the life of the town.

St. John's Park (about 1902)
This tiny cricket pavilion stood at the north-east corner of the park – within a stone's throw of St. John's Institute (Park Centre). From a social historian's point of view, it is interesting to note that the competing teams were labelled the 'Coachmen' and the 'Gardeners'. The umpire standing to the right of the photograph was Mr Tom Scrase, a veteran of the Boer War.

St. John's Park – the Peace-Day rejoicings
On 19th July, 1919, Burgess Hill honoured its heroes of the First World War, the living and the dead. It was hardly a time of rejoicing, more a moment of inexpressible sadness, an occasion that brought tears to the eyes of many who had gathered in the park.
Devotions and speeches were the order of the day, at the end of which, in a conscious effort to shake off the pervading gloom, the assembly made its way to the Victoria Pleasure Gardens, where Mr Street, his family and staff, awaited them with a celebratory dinner in the great hall.

St. John's Park (about 1937)
A sporting occasion held in the park; part of the town's celebrations in commemorating the coronation of George VI.
The boys in caps and white mackintoshes are from St. Luke's Home.
The building in the background, the Strict Baptists' Providence Chapel in Park Road, is now a private residence.

St. John's Park (about 1936)
Although a popular feature for many years, the boating and paddling pool had no filtering or circulating system. This became a cause of concern as it contravened health regulations, and after enquiring into the matter, the Authorities concluded that the cost of installing such equipment would be prohibitive. Better, they thought, to close it down, which is what occurred.

St. John's Park (about 1936)
Although less crowded than now, the view, despite the passage of years, remains much the same.
The pitch and putt.course was to the right of the central path.

St. John's Park (about 1935)
This photograph was taken shortly after the 'swimming pool in the park' had been opened. High diving boards and fountain were yet to be added. The venue, an immediate success, attracted great crowds and provided Mid Sussex generally and Burgess Hill in particular, with a sporting and fun facility previously undreamt of. The young lady facing the camera (bottom right) was Peggy Turner, née Skelhorn, who in later years was known to generations of local children as a 'Lollipop Lady' (Schools' Crossing Officer).

Lower Church Road, Burgess Hill, Sussex.

Lower Church Road

This fine photograph provides us with a glimpse of the area as it used to be when the western end of St. John's Park was still a meadow, and the pavement on the northern side of the road was lined with trees.

A glimpse between their trunks reveals plenty of activity beyond, as well as the broken iron fence referred to by Fitzharry.

The approaching horse and cart belonged to a local rag-and-bone man called 'Minker' Mitchell; he was also an unofficial supplier of game, and his cry in broad Sussex dialect of "Rabbits – Rabbits woild," was well known to the residents of Burgess Hill.

The lady with the crutch standing by her front garden gate, to the right of the picture, was Miss Jean Browning.

Lower Church Road, looking east (about 1920)
The milk float to the right of the photograph was from the Victoria Farm Dairy, a business owned by our grandfather and managed by his youngest son, Tom Street. The sliding doors in the premises behind the float opened to grandpa's slaughter house, and Teddy Alwen – he who was carried off by the pig, was the son of the baker on the other side of the road.

In the picture, the first floor window on the right hand side opened to Tom Street's bedroom, a scene of painful memory. During the course of an Easter weekend, he had agreed to assist Teddy with a morning delivery of hot cross buns. It required an early start and Tom was a heavy sleeper, so it was arranged that he should tie a piece of string around his big toe and suspend the other end through the window, then Teddy could pull it to wake his friend. Unfortunately he pulled too hard and nearly dislocated Tom's toe. The lad's cries of pain awoke the household and several weeks were to pass before he walked normally again.

Lower Church Road
Mr H. Hills for many years ran a greengrocery business which was situated near to the present day sub-post office. The wooden façade shown in this photograph has long since disappeared.

London Road is the main highway running through Burgess Hill, and leading off from this is Royal George Road, which takes us on the last leg of our journey.

A short distance along we pass Aberdeen Cottages, and it was there at number 6, many years ago, that the following incident (our final animal story) occurred.

Mrs Clarke of that address was enjoying a cup of tea when she heard a knock on the front door. Being that she was expecting company, she rose to her feet and with the words, "I am so glad to see you," framed on her lips, opened the door and beheld – a cow staring her in the face!

Then, according to the Mid Sussex Times:

> … the woman fled in terror, but the animal, struck by the attractiveness of the place, rushed indoors, going right through the front room and into the living room. Mrs Clarke raised the alarm at the house of a neighbour, Mr W. G. Pryor. "Oh, do come, there is a cow in my house," she gasped. Billy Pryor was not the sort to funk at a cow. He was quickly on the spot and found her ladyship playing all sorts of pranks with the happy home. "Come on, out of it," said Pryor, giving the cow a slap on the rump, but she simply replied with a whisk of her tail and a low "moo," thereby proclaiming herself the Mistress of the Ceremonies.

A table and all the tea things were overturned, amongst them, a lighted lamp, but this was grabbed in the nick of time by Mr Pryor, who was subsequently joined by Mr Packham in efforts to eject the animal.

The cow wanted to go upstairs to bed and felt insulted when the door was closed in her face! She let fly in all directions, and, finally, after creating a scene of chaos and excitement, was ignominiously backed out into free country.

Royal George Road
Mr George Coleman's shoe shop.

Edwin Street's butcher's shop (about 1924)
Our grandfather died in 1923, at which time his butchery business at the corner of Lower Church Road and London Road was inherited by his eldest son (also named Edwin). He is pictured here with his daughter, Daisy, and son – yet another Edwin – standing in front of the shop. With them is a young cousin, Ron Upton, and an employee, Mr Bill Woolven.
Of the many stories told concerning the premises, one featured a sword swallower. Apparently he was a member of a travelling fair and had called in to purchase some sausages, whereupon grandpa, obviously recognising the man, handed him an 18-inch sharpening steel, and joked, "Try swallowing this then". Taking the remark quite literally, the customer tilted back his head and lowered the instrument into his gullet. "Mmm," he remarked upon disgorging it, "that tasted nice and meaty".

Beyond Aberdeen Cottages we pass the entrance to Fairfield Road, where at one time, at what is now the junction with Gloucester Road, was parked a former railway guard's van, and in it, 'Frenchman' and his family lived. 'Frenchman,' 'Red Un,' 'Coxey' and 'Maggot' were all well known to the local constabulary and Haywards Heath magistrates.

Gregory, in 'The Story of Burgess Hill,' describes them as being 'characters'. Others regarded them as objectionable drunks, and in 1881, a newspaper item headed, 'A Burgess Hillian on the Spree,' tended to support their point of view:

> On Wednesday, at the Hove Police Court, George Waller, 44, better known as 'Frenchman,' an attendant of fairs and clubs with coconut shies, whelks and gingerbread, living at St. John's Common, Burgess Hill, was charged with being drunk and disorderly at Poynings on the 16th, and assaulting P.C. Gilbert.
>
> A festival was held at Poynings, prisoner being present, and having become intoxicated, played sundry capers, using most disgusting language, falling over a cart, interfering with everybody in general, and the policeman in particular, giving that functionary 'one in the eye'.
>
> On being taken into custody he varied his performances by dancing, kicking and rampaging about, until the assistance of a gardener named Hollingdale had been obtained.

Twelve months later, 'Frenchman' was passing Bank Buildings in his cart. He was carrying on in his usual drunken fashion, bawling and waving his arms about, when he overbalanced, fell out and struck his head on the highway. He died a few days later.

In a brief obituary, the Mid Sussex Times described him as a 'Huckster', and then went on to say:

> A deal of pity is felt for the poor fellow, as he was looked upon as a local celebrity, on account of his strange vagaries.

Those who at various times had been on the receiving end of the man's "strange vagaries" were probably less charitable in estimating his character.

Royal George Road
Mrs Eliza King, together with her husband and Miss Charity Allfrey (daughter by her first marriage), lived at Palm Cottage, the western-most of a pair of semi-detached properties that stood (and still stand) on the corner of Portland Road.
This photograph shows Mrs King at the front door, Mr King by the gate, and Charity Allfrey beside a huge tricycle.

Portland Road
At one time called 'The Den', Portland Road is a private thoroughfare that connects Royal George Road with London Road.
The lady seated on the right in the buggy is Mrs Eliza King, formerly Mrs Allfrey, née Avery. She was reputed to have owned all the property in the neighbourhood, and was required by law to close the lane one day a year, in order to preserve its status. Her daughter, Miss Charity Allfrey, is driving the carriage.

Royal George Road
Cricks Stores at the junction of Fairfield Road.
The land on the southern side of Royal George Road appears to be undeveloped, but appearances deceive, for Peartree Cottage, one of the oldest properties in Burgess Hill, lies to the left and out of the camera's view. Once on the edge of the town, it is now all but concealed in the heart of the Orchard Road estate.

Royal George Road looking west (about 1940)
This photograph was taken from a German Dornier en-route to bomb a specified target in Surrey.
Its reason for flying low over the town was because the railway junction south of Wivelsfield Station, and the tall chimneys of the Keymer Brick and Tile Works, provided unmistakable landmarks for the navigator. Townsfolk thought the aircraft was one of their own, and it was only when the large crosses on the wings became visible, and machine gun fire was directed at some of the buildings, that they dived for cover. Some of the shots ricocheted through the International Stores in Church Road, but nobody was hit.

To return to everyday matters, it is of interest to note that there were approximately 17 laundries engaged in or about Burgess Hill in 1900, which, with the possible exception of surrounding farms, made them the largest single group of businesses in the district.

There was a steam sanitary laundry, the Burgess Hill Steam Laundry, in Royal George Road. The proprietress, Mrs Lucy Chapman, described by Gregory as "that dear and kind hearted old lady," ran it very successfully for many years.

She started her washing career in Newport Road, then moved round the corner into London Road, and finally to Royal George Road, where a meadow between the buildings and the highway served as an excellent drying ground. To passers-by on a bright and breezy morning, the scene of billowing sheets tugging from the clothes lines was said to resemble a naval occasion at Portsmouth, or the Spithead Review!

At its peak the company was employing 100 workers, mostly women, and ran a collection and delivery service which extended as far as Brighton, Chailey and Ardingly.

Lucy Chapman's name first appeared as a laundress in the 1882 local directory, and it remained there until the late 1920s. Her husband, George Chapman, had little to do with the business. He was, at different times, a printer, a house agent, an auctioneer, furniture dealer and insurance representative. In other words, a man of many parts, although he wouldn't get his hands wet, he left that to his wife and sons, two of whom became directors of the company.

In 1945, farm workers on high land at Lodge Farm, Cuckfield, saw a black column of smoke belching out of a tall chimney in the vicinity of Burgess Hill and it soon became obvious that an entire structure was ablaze. The scene was not as they originally thought, one of the huge stacks at the Keymer Brick and Tile Works, but the laundry in Royal George Road, where, for some reason, the boiler house had gone up in flames.

The heat was intense and the danger considerable, but it did not deter Mr Frank Martin, the company's head van driver, from pluckily forcing open an office window and rescuing the firm's ledgers and petty cash. Yet despite his brave efforts, the buildings were completely gutted. A post fire assessment indicated that several months of renovation and replacement work would be required before the business was up and running again.

A rival establishment, the Mid Sussex Laundry Company, which operated out of Lindfield, offered to help until they were back on their feet, an offer that was gratefully accepted, and a number of the Burgess Hill staff transferred to the new premises where they were able to process and maintain a limited customer service.

While this was going on, the Royal George Road buildings were reconstructed on up-to-date lines: steel frames instead of wooden roof rafters and modern machinery to replace older equipment.

The Company re-opened in January, 1946, its slogan still, 'Let the laundry do it all,' and life returned to normal – but not for long. The local authorities had approved a proposal to build a factory estate on the site of the old Victoria Pleasure Gardens, which meant that more jobs with higher wages would soon be available to the townsfolk.

Royal George Road
We have been unable to glean any definite information about this photograph. Clearly it is to do with the Burgess Hill Steam Laundry, and therefore probably consists of Mrs Lucy Chapman and her family.
If our assumption is correct, then Mrs Chapman is surely seated third in from the left, with husband, George, standing second in from the right.

Barracks Cottages, Royal George Road
In the census of 1841, the Barracks was described as a block of farm workers' lodgings, housing five separate families (this number is believed to have increased to eight by 1851).
Built on land belonging to Gattens Farm, its original function (prior to the opening of the Union Workhouse at Cuckfield) was to provide accommodation for the 'poor and needy'. Burgess Hill Steam Laundry's chimney (the one that later caught fire) can be seen in the background.

Royal George Road
This photograph, taken from a first floor window at Springfield Terrace, shows riders on the way to a meet of the Southdown Hunt, held either at West End Farm, or the Magpie Public House (now the Sportsman), Goddards Green.
The gate in the foreground closes off the track to Colmer Place, while the white lane running across the meadow, leads to Erin Manor. Peartree Cottage may be seen on the near horizon to the left of the picture, otherwise it is only fields.

Royal George Road
A team of haymakers at work in a meadow belonging to Fowels Farm. The farmhouse, no longer named as such, is with us still, but the surrounding fields are buried beneath the Orchard Road estate. The building (centre background) was Southdown House.

Royal George Road
Another view of haymaking. We have been informed by an old Burgess Hillian, that the workman seated on the rake was Mr Charlie Pierce.

New government regulations were imposing higher costs on employers. And, the biggest blow of all, electrically operated washing machines were becoming generally available for domestic use.

Although good news for the public at large, the combination of these events proved disastrous for outfits like Lucy Chapman's laundry. It soldiered on for a while, but the end was in sight, and by 1967 the little Burgess Hill company had washed its last shirt, pressed its last collar and closed its doors for good.

Hidden from view in our photographs stands Fowels Farm (now called Old Timbers) and from research we have discovered that in the early 19th century the place was the residence of Alan and Sarah Avery. Their daughter, Ann, an emotionally unstable young lady, married Charles Tulley of Scotches Farm, Hurstpierpoint, and in due course they had a son, also named Charles. Then tragedy struck, for a few days after his birth, Ann, who had been behaving most peculiarly, was discovered drowned in the nearby mill-pond.

Charles Tulley senior, quite unable to look after a baby and run a farm, handed the little fellow over to his mother-in-law, who, having just given birth to another child of her own, a boy named John, was happy to raise the youngsters as brothers, although strictly speaking they were nephew and uncle.

At the age of 12, both lads left home in search of work, and Charles, with whom we are mainly concerned, became a butcher's boy in Brighton where he worked a 12-hour day for 6 days a week. That he worked hard at his career is shown by the fact that while still a very young man, he returned to Burgess Hill to open up a butchers shop of his own.

St. Edward's Chapel (about 1968)

The bricklayer, Mr R. Winter, is the only person who appears to be working here. He is being watched by Mr Harry Stoner and two young apprentices, J. Faulkner and C. Chapman.

When completed, their labours resulted in the Chapel being consecrated as a fully fledged, albeit subsidiary, church to St. John's. It was not until the year 2000 that St. Edward's threw off the yoke and received parish status in its own right.

In the graveyard beyond, a tombstone engraved with a shepherd marks the last resting place of one of Mid Sussex's best remembered tradesmen, Mr Antonio Faccenda. He was a manufacturer and purveyor of 'Hoky Poky' ice cream, a product that was consumed in great quantities by visitors to the local Victoria Pleasure Gardens, as well as the Chinese Gardens at Hurstpierpoint, and the Orchard Tea Gardens at Hassocks.

Mr Faccenda's ice cream cart was a familiar sight in the district, but one to watch out for if you were wise, as on a certain occasion, the horse bolted down Livingstone Road, straight across the Royal George Road, with the cart ending up on its side in the front garden of 6 Menin Gate Terrace. Ice cream and money were scattered everywhere. Local children were quickly at the scene, and it speaks highly of their honesty that every penny was returned.

'Stop Me and Buy One' was Mr Faccenda's slogan, and people needed little persuasion.

Royal George Road
This is Berry's Brickyard whilst it was still a manufacturing unit, and all those in the group appear to be holding the tools or produce of their trade. With this in mind, it is perhaps of interest to note that the man on the left is clutching a huge brick or block of some sort, an item that looks to be fairly heavy. If such was the case, one can only marvel at the strength of his companion with the cart!
The buildings in the background face on to West Street, and the location of Downs Road is clearly visible.

The business succeeded beyond Tulley's wildest dreams, to such an extent that he found himself in a position to invest in his real love, livestock and land, ventures that proved to be equally successful. Indeed it seemed as if he possessed the Midas touch, as in an incredibly short time, this man who had once struggled through Brighton's streets carrying carcases of meat on his back for only one shilling a week, came to own West End Farm, a thriving butcher's shop, and a valuable interest in a local brick manufacturing company.

That was not all. In 1840, the London to Brighton railway was being constructed, an event which offered great opportunities for those with vision and the financial wherewithal. Charles saw a niche in the market and supplied timber, mainly from his own land, to be used as sleepers. And his delivery carts never returned empty, but were filled with chalk that had been excavated from Clayton Tunnel. This was used for road making and other building purposes.

In 1845, he married his cousin, Esther Avery, and as if to prove his energies were not confined to money-making, fathered 12 children, all of whom were well provided for.

An example of his generosity is the property that stands at the corner of Stanford Avenue and the western approach to Hassocks railway station. After demolishing a warehouse that originally stood on the site, he built a shop with residential accomodation (a late wedding gift) for his youngest daughter, Patience, and her husband, Israel Avery, who happened to be his nephew. A plaque bearing the inscription, "C.T. 1896," can be seen on the wall of the building to this day in recognition of his generosity.

West End Farm (about 1900)
Once a rural outpost of Burgess Hill, now the fields and woods of Charles Tulley's day are buried beneath bricks and mortar, while his old home, which still stands, has been converted into a public house called the Woolpack.

Charles Tulley, a noted sheep breeder who still worked for six hours a day at the age of 102, and claimed to have over 200 descendents scattered all over the Empire and the United States of America; who in addition to his butchery, brickmaking and building interests, farmed over 2,000 acres of prime Sussex land at West End, Pangdean and Poynings, died in his 103rd year, and is buried in the little churchyard of St. John the Baptist at Clayton.

From the former Fowels Farm to St. Edward's Church is only a brief stroll, with houses all the way. We mention this because, at one time, and certainly within living memory, the district was virtually rural, consisting of meadow, hedgerow and wide open spaces. The church is a modern building, and one that owes its position to a problem which concerned Burgess Hill in the early years of the 20th century, much as it concerns us today (2003) – and that is, the lack of sufficient burial space.

Then, the matter was solved by a great benefactor to the district, Mr A. J. Bridge of Wyberlye, who, in memory of his late wife, presented the town with nearly three acres of land.

The ground, formerly part of Berry's Brickyard at the western end of Royal George Road, was consecrated as a graveyard in 1920.

In 1936, St. Edward's Chapel, given by Miss Gertrude Holbeache in memory of her brother, was erected on the site, and in 1968, it was enlarged and consecrated as a subsidiary to St. John's; while in the year 2000 the building became the parish church of St. Edward's in its own right.

The brickfield (Berry's) extended across the land separating Royal George Road from West Street, and stretched eastwards to Downs Road, although nowadays there is little to show that it ever existed.

When the clay was exhausted and the workmen had left, nature took over and transformed the site into a wilderness of uneven hillocks, clumps of gorse and narrow footpaths leading in all directions.

Little creatures sheltered amongst tangled thickets, or in some rusty iron rails, twisted together like enormous strands of spaghetti, while tumbledown walls smothered with dog rose and bindweed, provided a haven for tiny birds, lizards and all manner of interesting insects.

Known as the 'Brickie' it was a sort of wild park, a haunt of local children, many of whom, now in their advancing years, still recall the place with affection.

And it is at the 'Brickie,' which remains a recreational area, but one that has become bland and civilised and not at all as we described, that our journey comes to its end.

ALSO AVAILABLE FROM MID SUSSEX BOOKS

Edwin Street and the Victoria Pleasure Gardens
Mark Dudeney and Eileen Hallett

From Pyecombe to Cuckfield
Mark Dudeney and Eileen Hallett

Albourne to Ditchling: Along the Greensand Ridge
Mark Dudeney and Eileen Hallett

The Pleasure Grounds of Sussex
Mark Dudeney and Eileen Hallett

In Preparation
The Old Century
Mark Dudeney

Also published
Autobiography of George Mockford

Mark Dudeney has also written for W.H. Smith
Burgess Hill: Living Memories of your Town